Everyday Matters

Words of Life

Sandy Popp

LION HEARTS PRESS

Copyright Page

Lion Hearts Press in Boerne, Texas
Copyright ©2025 by Sandy Popp
All rights reserved. No part of this publication may be reproduced, stored in a retrieval system or transmitted in any form by any means, electronic, mechanical, photocopy recording, or otherwise without prior written permission of the publisher.

Editor: Robin Carpio
Proofread & Copy Edits: Robin Carpio
Cover photography: Chase Ryan of Ryan River Media
Interior design and typesetting: Sandy Popp & Robin Carpio

Scripture quotations marked (NIV) are taken from the Holy Bible, New International Version®, NIV®. Copyright © 1973, 1978, 1984, 2011 by Biblica, Inc.™ Used by permission of Zondervan. All rights reserved worldwide. www.zondervan.com The "NIV" and "New International Version" are trademarks registered in the United States Patent and Trademark Office by Biblica, Inc.™

Interior Graphics licensed for use:
Images from "The Fruitful Tree" (tree), "Winter's Shroud" (snowy winter scene), "Happy Palm Sunday" (palm tree), "Mercy Flows" (waterfall), "Rocky is the Bitter Road" (rocky mountain scene) sourced from Chase Ryan at Ryan River Media
Image from "Child Warrior" (child in the forest) by Sarah Popp
Image from "Prayer for My Child" (pregnant mom) by Natalie Randall
Decorative flourish used in this book is created by Healltica Studio and sourced via Canva. Used with permission under Canva's content license.

ISBN: 978-0-9724140-4-3

For information on other publications by Sandy Popp,
visit us at www.sandypopp.com

Dedication

I dedicate this book to my loving Lord and Savior, who gave me the heart to pray for others and then put these poems on my heart. I'm in awe that You bless me despite my many shortcomings.

In loving memory of my father Skip Carr, who taught me how to be courageous.

Acknowledgements

My amazing husband, his brilliant mind and inspirational determination to meet life's challenges head-on. I'm grateful for his sacrifices and patience as I relearned MS Word crossing the finish line of this book.

My children and their loves—thank you for your support, belief in me, and, most of all, your love. And to my little Ela, the joy of my life.

A special thanks to my son, a gifted photographer, for the stunning cover image and other pictures in this book.

My mother, Pat Carr, a living reflection of God's love and mercy. To my big brother, Randy—your quick wit and protectiveness are a treasure—and to his wonderful wife, Anne.

My editor, Robin Carpio—thank you for the late nights, big and small decisions, prayers, shared laughter and snarky memes.

Table 5 ladies' Bible study group—your prayers and encouragement have been a steady source of support. I truly appreciate you.

My pastor, Max Lucado, whose ability to express God's grace with poetic elegance and down-to-earth wisdom continually inspires me to write better.

My Beta Readers—Pat Carr, Frankee Perry, Robin Carpio, Monte Klossen Michelle Rigsby, Margaret Wallace, Gloria Moran, Amelie Randall, Tanya Harper, and Kim Nichols—thank you for reading through countless unedited poems and helping shape this collection.

Before You Read

Some people feel a calling to pray for others. In many faith traditions, we are known as "intercessors"—those who lift others in prayer, asking God to intervene in their lives. When we pray for others, we follow Jesus' example by introducing God's presence and power in their lives.

When I intercede, a Scripture often comes to mind. Other times, my prayers take the form of poetry—what I call devotional or intercessory poetry. Some have called it prophetic poetry. Many have told me they feel God is speaking to them when they read it. This book is a collection of those sacred reflections and my personal prayers. Some were written in awe of God's power and kindness, others in moments of struggle and surrender.

I believe poetry is an often overlooked way God speaks to us. He has always used imagery, rhythm, and metaphor to reveal His truth. Some verses in this book may read as though God Himself is speaking—I take the liberty to do so because my words are drawn from the Bible, His words. However, they are paraphrased and woven into verse as I feel the impression of God's heart in response to life's realities.

As you turn these pages, I pray you hear His voice and feel His love and care.

Much love and many blessings,
Sandy

Table of Contents

HE SPEAKS 1
    OVERWHELMED 2
    TROUBLE TO TRIUMPH 4
    BEYOND MEASURE 5
    MISTAKES 6
    LISTEN 8
    MULTIPLY 9
    NEVER LEFT 10
    THE ARK 11
    DREAMS, DESTINY, AND POWER 12

CREATION SPEAKS 13
    WELCOME SPRING 14
    THE FRUITFUL TREE 15
    CONSIDER THE BIRDS 16
    WELCOME THE RAIN 17
    HIGH TIDE 18
    THE CLAY 20
    YOUR BEAUTIFUL REEL 21
    WINTER'S SHROUD 22

TIMES & SEASONS 23
    NEW 24
    PASSOVER (GOD'S LIBERAL GRACE) 25
    HAPPY PALM SUNDAY 26
    HIS SMILE 28
    FREEDOM RINGS 29
    EVERYTHING BUT JESUS 30
    HEAVEN'S GIFT 32
    SENT TO THE HUMBLE 34
    THE GREATEST NEWS 36

PRODIGAL JOURNEYS 37
    PRODIGAL'S SONG 38
    THE WANDERING SHEEP 39
    SHAKING LEGS 40
    THE BATTLE OF THE MIND 42
    WANTING IT TO END 44
    MERCY FLOWS 46
    IT'S NO SMALL THING 47

UNTIL YOU CALL ME HOME 48

LOVE & FRIENDSHIP 49
WHAT LOVE IS 50
ROCKY IS THE BITTER ROAD 51
YOU CAN'T MAKE THEM LOVE YOU 52
PRAYER FOR MY FRIEND 54
FORGIVEN 55
THE LEDGE 56
SNOBBERY ROBBERY 58
NO LOVE GREATER 60
POLITICAL DIVIDES 62

FAMILY & CHILDREN 63
A TOUCH OF HEAVEN 64
GIVEN 65
ABOVE RUBIES 66
NEWLYWED SONG 67
PRAYER FOR MY CHILD 68
BLOOM 69
CHILD WARRIOR 70
MOMMY, DO YOU LOVE ME? 71
MY PRODIGAL LOVE 72

SICKNESS, DEATH & HEAVEN 73
THROUGH THE VALLEY (PSALM 23) 74
IT'S NOT OVER 75
WALKING THROUGH 76
THE GOOD FIGHT 78
LIVE THOUGH WE DIE 79
HEAVEN'S SWEET REUNION 80
REMEMBER ME 82
WHERE THE SUN NEVER SETS 83
LAST BREATH 84

SALVATION MESSAGE & PRAYER 85

He Speaks

When We...

feel anxiety and stress.	p.2
are going through troubled times.	p.4
need help to take a step of faith.	p.5
struggle with the guilt of a mistake.	p.6
want to know what God might want.	p.8
need God to multiply our efforts.	p.9
need assurance God is with us.	p.10
need help trusting God in the storm.	p.11
worry about God's plans for our future.	p.12

Overwhelmed

Lord, I come before You
My plate is full and cracked.
Unsure of what to tackle
To get myself on track.

Everywhere I look
There's something I must do.
Oh God, it's never-ending
Help me find an end in You.

I need Your mighty wisdom
To prioritize my life.
A strategy and plan
To free me from this strife.

It's beyond my strength
To get all this in order.
I feel I need a miracle,
To set some peaceful borders.

My Child

Lay aside each weight
That stresses and ensnares.
Get up and run the race
Know that I am there.

Dig up the bitter roots
Put My cloak of power on.
Be ruthless with your idols
Cut ties until they're gone.

What you see around you
Is a picture of your soul.
Put your mind on Me
And focus on My goals.

Then things of earth will lose their lure
You'll walk in freedom's power.
Know that when you asked,
I began the work that hour.

"Since the first day that you set your mind to gain understanding and to humble yourself before your God, your words were heard, and I have come in response to them." Daniel 10:12 NIV

Trouble to Triumph

Trouble comes, and then it goes
It feeds our doubts, fears, and woes,
But wisdom's fruit will help us see
That blessings come from tragedy.

My Child

I'm good in both the rain and shine
Trials don't change this love of Mine.
For in each life, pain shall come
It only stops when life is done.

My steady grace is always there
It might be veiled behind your cares.
Bring them to the foot of the cross
And You'll see My love within your loss.

The rain will fall; the earth will groan
But in your heart, make Me a throne.
I can turn trouble to triumph; you'll see.
Nothing's impossible when you give it to Me.

*"As for you, you meant evil against me, but God meant it for good,
to save many people alive, as is happening today."*
Exodus 50:20 WEB

Beyond Measure

Test Me and see
If I'll come through.
You are Mine
And I care for you.

I see your need;
I hear your cry.
I am your guard;
Lift up your eyes.

Into My hands
Commit your treasure,
And I'll bless your life
Beyond all measure.

"Test me in this," says the Lord Almighty," and see if I will not throw open the floodgates of heaven and pour out so much blessing that there will not be room enough to store it." Malachi 3:10 NIV

Mistakes

I'm twisted up in torment
When I make a dumb mistake.
Judgmental thoughts, bring shame
And they're impossible to shake.

Lord, You're God above
I call now on Your name.
For all that I can feel is
Regret and woeful shame.

When can I be free, my God
From this yoke of sin?
Can you take this from me
So I'll feel peace again?

My Child

My child, you are troubled
By many painful things.
With shame, guilt, and stress
The devil plucks your strings.

Though you feel so helpless
Just look up and find My grace.
I'll be with you always
In everything you face.

Receive My love and know
That it will cover you.
Please give Me your mistakes
And trust My word is true.

Give to Me this debt and weight
Let doubts and fears subside.
Walk in the sweet assurance
That I won't leave your side.

"He will again have compassion on us. He will tread our iniquities under foot. You will cast all their sins into the depths of the sea."
Micah 7:19 WEB

Listen

I'm the loving Lord
The Creator of all,
With a masterful plan
For your life and call.

Hear it and heed it,
Don't turn away.
Salvation's appointed
On this very day.

Through others, My word,
Situations and dreams,
I give power and wisdom
To all who claim need.

My wisdom is free.
My heart is true.
Listen for Me
I'm here for you.

All who will seek,
Shall surely find.
If you learn My word
You'll know My mind.

"For everyone who asks receives; the one who seeks finds; and to the one who knocks, the door will be opened." Matthew 7:8 NIV

Multiply

Let Me work My grace in you
Mighty change is found in truth.
When you learn to first receive
Others will see this and then believe.

My love is true; I bring no harm
You are safe within My arms.
The gifts I have are free for the taking
Courage grows while you are shaking.

Don't look back; step as I lead
Just play your part and plant the seeds.
I'll keep them safe; I've heard your cry
The crop you plant, I'll multiply.

"You have not held back your son, your only son. So I will certainly bless you. I will make the children born into your family as many as the stars in the sky. I will make them as many as the grains of sand on the seashore. They will take over the cities of their enemies."
Genesis 22:16-17 NIV

Never Left

He's our help in troubled times
That's how the scripture goes.
It's sometimes hard to see
When in a sea of woes.

But God, in His kind mercy
Comes down to comfort us.
Although, at times, we feel alone
And our burdens weigh too much.

But God Almighty has the power
To give us strength and help.
We cry to Him, He rescues us
From our trials and ourselves.

But sometimes, in the middle
Of life's most trying times.
He doesn't seem to answer
My prayers and desperate cries.

In the lonely silence,
His answer is, "I'm here.
I will walk you through this
Because I hold you dear."

"Though you feel alone
You don't need to run or hide.
It may feel unbearable,
I'm right here by your side."

"When this time is over
And you stand on peaceful sands.
You'll see My love was faithful
And you've never left My hands."

" Know therefore that the LORD your God is God; he is the faithful God." Deuteronomy 7:9 NIV

The Ark

Pushed on every side with pressure, pain, and sorrow
Grasping for the light, with hope to see tomorrow.
As troubles swell and dwarf my soul
My life is spinning out of control.

Though terror is knocking, I hear a sweet sound
The voice of my King on the sea, not the ground.
Through the wind and the waves, He peacefully strides
He longs for my soul, which both stands and hides.

"Come to Me," He says with outstretched hands
Mine are the footprints throughout your life's sands.
I have walked with you always, now come with me
I have peace for you in these stormy seas.

Look into My eyes, see My face, know My heart
In trusting Me, you build an ark.
As Noah was spared from the ruin of flood,
Your salvation comes in My Son's precious blood.

As hell's fury rages, I will stay true
Nothing's stronger than My love for you.
I give peace to your soul and My healing balm
Though the storms will rage, you will be calm.

I came to bring you closer to Me,
For your sins and burdens, I hung on that tree.
Accept this gift from the lover of your soul
You're safe in Me, and I won't let you go.

"Come," he said. Then Peter got down out of the boat, walked on the water and came toward Jesus." Matthew 14:29 NIV

Dreams, Destiny, and Power

I have plans for you, My child
Don't let heart and mind run wild.
Take some time and learn My heart
This is where your destiny starts.

You are My child; you have My love
I treasure you from above.
Don't think I won't or that I can't
You'll find grace within My hands.

Dare to believe, oh, child of Mine
Take hold of Me and cross the lines.
Cross lines of fear and of dismay
Dare to believe, and I'll make a way.

"In him we are also chosen, not having been predestined according to a plan of him who works out everything in conformity with the purpose of his will." Ephesians 1:11 NIV

Creation Speaks

To one who...

wants to see God in the spring.	p.14
is worried that growth is taking too long.	p.15
needs assurance of God's provision.	p.16
wants to see God in the rain.	p.17
deals with a lot of anxiety.	p.18
wants God's help to change.	p.20
struggles with comparison.	p.21
needs to see God in the winter.	p.22

Welcome Spring

Lift your eyes to the hills; don't grope in the dark,
Search for the Lord; He has hope for your heart.
In His powerful grace, sunlight abounds,
He's a vision of spring with His sights and sounds.

The jubilant flowers; the birds' sweet songs,
Cue winter's demise, dark and prolonged.
Hope springs alive so open up your eyes
His mercy is vast as a sunny spring sky.

His grace is steady; He never changes
Though our sinful hearts, He rearranges.
Each morning is new, ripe on the vine
For each of us He makes it shine.

Though I have wavered and fallen down
He's still willing to give me His crown.
God, You are Lord, Christ and King,
My life was the winter; You are my spring.

Into my darkness, You brought the light
Out of sure death, You produced life.
You make fruitful that which was dead
You give me joy where I had only dread.

'I lift up my eyes to the mountains where does my help come from My help comes from the Lord, the Maker of heaven and earth.."
Psalm 121:1-2 NIV

The Fruitful Tree

I looked in wonder and did see
A freshly planted apple tree.
It was small and had no fruit
Yet promise waits within the root.

It had no fear of rot or spoil
It just grew strong in God's rich soil.
In winter, spring, summer, and fall
The tree kept slowly growing tall.

When, at last, the fruit did come
It wasn't ripe, or sweet, or plump.
The tree stood tall without a fear
Waiting for its time of year.

Then one day the fruit was ripe;
The tree spent not one day in strife.
It took in the sun, it drank from soil,
And God brought growth without one toil.

Each year the seeds are newly sown
And with no stress, they simply grow.
The job of the tree is just to be
And time brings gifts of maturity.

Fruit swells big as the tree grows strong
And the rich, ripe fruit is a victory song.
God teaches us through a simple tree
Don't stress; you'll grow when you receive.

"If that is how God clothes the grass of the field, which is here today and tomorrow is thrown into the fire, will he not much more clothe you —you of little faith?" Matthew 6:30 NIV

Consider the Birds

They come and visit every day
Without a care or worry.
They eat their fill and sing their songs
Until the winter finds its fury.

They care not what tomorrow brings
They think only of today.
They live their lives with songs of joy
As God leads them on their way.

They fret not for their daily bread
They never stress or fear.
God provides and always meets
Their needs throughout the year.

What lesson does our Maker want
To teach us through the birds?
They worry not, yet He provides
As He promised in His word.

So sing your song of joy to Him
Ban anxiousness and fear.
Search and work; let God provide
Each season of the year.

"See the birds of the sky, that they don't sow, neither do they reap, nor gather into barns. Your heavenly Father feeds them. Aren't you of much more value than they?" Matthew 6:26 WEB

Welcome The Rain

The rain sings praise of spring's new birth
It streams from heaven, and soaks the earth.
The sun sits veiled behind dark clouds
They cover the earth like a burial shroud.

The birds and the fauna all hide away
Huddled in hope for the next sunny day.
People rush by all covered and bleak
Running through life like shepherd-less sheep.

Rain pours to the ground and doesn't relent
Fulfilling the purpose for which it was sent.
It heals and restores the cracked, dry land
It brings provision from God's mighty hand.

It unlocks nutrition from the lowly dirt
Releasing the treasures inside hidden earth.
The earth is changed by the long, heavy rain
For the darkness of storms is never in vain.

Nature rejoices with color, texture, and flower
Beauty supplants all that was sour.
We were dry and cracked, lifeless and hard
God's beauty blooms where hope was charred.

Life feels unjust when we're pelted by storms
But God doesn't hate us; this isn't His scorn.
Let our roots grow deep when the rains increase
And we will then bloom by the grace of our King.

"As the rain and snow come down from heaven and do not return to it without watering the earth and making it flourish so my word that goes out from my mouth, it will not return to me empty."
Isaiah 55: 10-11 NIV

High Tide

Moment by moment, I'm still overthrown
Overwhelmed by it all, I feel so alone.
Moment by moment, I'll trust in Your grace
It's all I can manage with all that I face.

You don't expect me to do this alone
Your wings: my cover, Your grace: my home.
All that I care for, I trust You to keep
I will trust in you and peacefully sleep.

God, my new worries weigh so much more
What do I do as I stand on this shore?
My nets are empty; my body is weak
I can't seem to manage one more thing.

The waves rise high in the threatening sea
I fear they will drown or swallow me.
Will You be there to catch what I drop?
When will this torrent of trouble stop?

My Child

I was there on the top of your soaring heights
I'm here with you now in the darkest of nights.
When you walk through this water, I will be there
Cast on Me your fears and your cares.

You can't control this, as you see
I keep all that you give to Me.
If you fear, get mad, fail, and doubt
I will never cast you out.

You can't get credit when this is done
But they'll look at you and see the Son.
Through the fire, I'll walk with you
I died for your sin; what won't I do?

Look up to the hills for help from your Lord
Let My Spirit comfort; be led by My word.
Cast thoughts of dread and cares on Me
You aren't alone, just lean on Me.

*"I will lift up my eyes to the hills. Where does my help come from?
My help comes from Yahweh, who made heaven and earth."
Psalm 121:1 WEB*

The Clay

Make me a vessel that brings You glory
Let my life reflect Your pure love story.
Hone my soul, and cleanse my heart.
Let no blemish stay; let today be the start.

Mold me, oh Lord, to be just like You
Let my heart echo Your mercy and truth.
From this humble place, I willingly bow
I yield my heart to the work of Your plow.

Help me to purge the weeds, clumps, and rocks;
Give me the courage and strength to stop.
To stop habits that harm and desires to sin
That imprison my soul time and again.

Make me an instrument worthy to speak
Of Your mighty love and the wisdom I seek.
May my witness be strong, my words be true
Let all I accomplish bring glory to You.

"Yet you, Lord, are our Father.
We are the clay, you are the potter;
we are all the work of your hand. Isaiah 64:8 NIV

Your Beautiful Reel

How pretty, lovely, and perfect you are,
I love to watch all that you do.
But how can I even come close,
To being as perfect as you?

I try hard to reach up,
And to make myself great,
But I always fall short.
Is "average" my fate?

What I see are your highlights,
It's not all that you are.
It's filtered and polished with edits,
But it's still my impossible bar.

I must realize as I step away,
That I, too, am a beautiful treasure.
Not glossy or crowned for a reel,
But valued beyond earthly measure.

For I'm made just like me for a reason,
My piece in life's puzzle profound.
I complete my part of the world,
And that's why my place must be found.

I'm not you, so I must find,
My purpose in God's perfect plan.
I can learn from your beautiful reel,
But You celebrate who I am.

"For we are his workmanship, created in Christ Jesus for good works, which God prepared before that we would walk in them."
Ephesians 2:10 WEB

Winter's Shroud

The silence of winter is chillingly loud;
Nature seems muted in a cold, icy shroud.
The past life of summer, the brilliance of fall
Are encrypted in white, which covers it all.

There's a newness within fresh, fallen snow,
The once brilliant fall, now a colorless glow.
All hidden formations in pallets of white,
Boast only broad strokes of nature's might.

It's time to dream and to fill in the lines,
Simplicity reigns within wintery whites.
It's a time to be tranquil like the nature around,
To reflect, plan, and relish the lovely profound.

It's a time to be still and let God draw near,
And ask for His vision for the upcoming year.
Be silent, be placid, give God the reigns
And bury the past with its victories and pain.

Be still like the winter and let wisdom glow
Give to God your hardness of soul.
The death of winter feeds the newness of spring.
It reminds us that God loves to do new things.

---

*"It was you who set all the boundaries of the earth;
you made both summer and winter." Psalm 74:17 NIV*

Times &

Seasons

A Time To...

consider new year beginnings.	p.24
reflect on Passover.	p.25
explore Palm Sunday.	p.26
meditate on Jesus' thoughts of the cross.	p.28
celebrate Independence Day.	p.29
put Christ back in Christmas.	p.30
reminisce on the first Christmas gift.	p.32
see Christ's birth with the Shepard's eyes.	p.34
consider God's priorities.	p.36

New

I'm doing a new thing; can you perceive it?
Try with your might to simply believe it.
Don't look to the past, disappointments and fears
I can do a new thing in this brand-new year.

Embrace your hope, and do not shrink.
You can walk on the water and not sink.
You've been oppressed and held in vain.
A seed of faith will make a change.

I'll save you and place you on steady ground
Though you are trapped by many self-doubts.
Stretch out your faith; look up and believe
Just open your heart and, in faith, receive.

Oh, how I love you, child of Mine.
Life on earth will rarely be fine,
But give to Me your heart's desire.
And let Me fill it with holy fire.

Prepare some room to receive Me today
Give Me your plans, and I'll guide your way.
I'll never give up, and I'll make your life new
The bloodstained cross is the burden of proof.

"Behold, I will do a new thing. It springs out now. Don't you know it? I will even make a way in the wilderness, and rivers in the desert."
Isaiah 43:19 WEB

Passover (God's Liberal Grace)

The night of the howling wind crept by
As we heard the hearts of our neighbor's cry.
Firstborn were taken throughout the town
Havoc is now the song that resounds.

We had huddled with hope behind our doors
With a shield of blood and nothing more.
Reciting our prayers by dim candlelight
With unnatural peace that held our faith tight.

Morning saw cries for loved one's friends
The unprepared souls met bitter ends.
A stark reminder of God's might and love
That life is held in the power of the blood.

Those holding us captive met terrible fates
Reaping their fruit of violence and hate.
They gave us their spoils and set us free
To a hot desert land through a crimson sea.

Deliverance came in the blood of the lamb
And not through might or works of man.
It speaks of the Savior that would die in our place
So our sins would be covered by God's liberal grace.

The Passover time is sweet news to me
It's a powerful message to all who will see.
Our ransom paid by the Lamb that was slain
So that we can live within heaven's reign.

"The next day, he saw Jesus coming to him, and said, "Behold, the Lamb of God, who takes away the sin of the world!" John 1:29 WEB

Happy Palm Sunday

I wished you a happy Palm Sunday, Lord
But on thinking, my heart grows heavy.
This is the day they waved their palms
While You came to them on a donkey.

An ambassador King, You came in peace
Though You could have entered in power.
You gave Your grace to the least of the least
As You prepared for that fateful hour.

How could Your heart not be weighted
As You rode on the path of their best?
For You knew those crying "Hosanna"
Would soon shout out loud for Your death.

How can this day be happy and joyous
When it stands for pain and betrayal?
With joyful vision, You rode to Your fate
To provide us a place at Your table.

That's why You're God, and we are not
It was only You who could come.
For humanity was bit with the curse of sin
Only You could render undone.

How did you do it, my God and King
Knowing they'd soon want Your death?
How did you not despise their cheers
Then forgive them with Your dying breath?

It was Your purpose in coming to earth
To walk among humans, You made.
To show the heart of a generous God
Then pay our price to be saved.

I lift my heart and psalms of praise
For this happy Sunday of palms.
For it stands for the start of the end of the curse
And the promise of Your open arms.

"A very great multitude spread their clothes on the road. Others cut branches from the trees and spread them on the road. The multitudes who went in front of him, and those who followed, kept shouting, "Hosanna! to the son of David! Blessed is he who comes in the name of the Lord! Hosanna in the highest!" Matthew 21:8-9 WEB

His Smile

The clamoring crowd pushes and fights
To sing the praise and see the sight.
As He rides through town on a beast of peace
Not an earthly rex, but the King of Kings.

He knows that their love is only skin-deep
Their cheers are the neighs of well-meaning sheep.
Yet He rides through a shallow homage of palms
With His eyes alight as they sing heaven's songs.

Such a joy-filled procession on a glorious day
Singing Hosanna, do they know what they say?
Do they see the price of the salvation they seek?
The praise turned to scorn as He hung from a tree.

He knows it's the cross at the end of this road
It's the price He must pay for our heavy sin load.
He knows that this day, with these elated cheers
Will be rivaled by hate on His cross of tears.

His smile wasn't because of their praise
But for the fruit of the price He'll pay:
For His purpose served, and humanity saved
Put light in His eyes and the smile on His face.

"Looking to Jesus, the author, and perfecter of faith, who for the joy that was set before him endured the cross, despising its shame, and has sat down at the right hand of the throne of God." Hebrews 12:2 WEB

Freedom Rings

Courage paved a crimson path,
Released from fear of monarch wrath.
Filled with hope on gleaming shores;
Free from fighting voiceless wars.

Let's esteem God-given rights;
Embrace with joy a happy life.
Let's prize the fight that made us free,
That gave us life and liberty.

Let's scorn constraints of despot ways,
Unoccupied by hate or frays.
'Till freedom rings throughout our land,
For each woman, child, and man.

"Now the Lord is the Spirit, and where the Spirit of the Lord is, there is freedom." 2 Corinthians 3:17 NIV

Everything But Jesus

I hung up my Christmas lights
And decked my house and yard.
I wrote the yearly letter
For my Christmas cards.

I bought the cheery paper
To wrap presents from my lists,
But there's more sales and deals
That I really can't resist.

I planned my celebrations
I baked Christmas treats galore.
I'm pushed beyond my limits
Yet there's always more.

Pageants, plays, and parties
To each, I bring a present.
When the bills start rolling in
I'll be living like a peasant.

I delight in my good recipes
In my garlands and my bows,
But hold my breath until it's done
And life begins to slow.

There is something I'm forgetting
Amidst all my tasks and chores,
As the Reason this exists at all
Knocks at my festive door.

Yet merrily I dance along to
The songs of this great season.
Busied with the trappings
And forgetting He's the reason.

What does God in Heaven think
When in His name that freed us.
Our busyness and mounting debt
Praises everything but Jesus?

"...and the cares of this age, and the deceitfulness of riches, and the lusts of other things entering in choke the word, and it becomes unfruitful." Mark 4:19 WEB

Heaven's Gift

Undeserved, yet unapplauded
God's gift to wayward man.
Bestowed in silent secrecy
To tiny, hallowed hands.

Shepherds arrested by heavenly hosts
Proclaiming God's grace wasn't far.
Prophesies hung in the heavens
Kings followed the foretold star.

A scene of serene glory,
The weight of a holy hush.
The meaning of Heaven's story,
Was God's Christmas gift to us.

Who would recall the power of that day,
God's gift emerged through sacred womb.
Then to a cross He was led away,
To bear a crown, a robe, and our wounds,

Shall we turn from the holy blessing
And walk away unchanged?
Will we let it envelope our souls
Then allow it to slip away?

Through plastic, tinsel, parties, and gifts
Can this endowment be heard or seen?
In shopping, planning, and Christmas lights lit,
Is it shrouded by frantic, holiday sheen?

Let us not forget, God showed His love
Through the power of His sacrifice.
It's advent sweet, it's ending harsh,
To forgive and cleanse and give us life.

Will we take and relish His mighty gift
Or let our sense of the manger wane?
The touch of heaven is ours to receive
When we embrace the reason He came.

Hand painted by Mom

"For God so loved the world, that he gave his one and only Son..."
John 3:16 NIV

Sent to the Humble

'Twas an everyday night like so many before.
'Twas an average day of labor and chores.
We kept the sheep alone on the hills
While trying to shed the late evening chills.

A sudden light, then a glorious song
Filled the lost, forsaken, poor, and wronged.
The weight of heaven's beauty and power
Surrounded us that very hour.

The sky did shine; the trumpets did sound.
And a host of angels did surround.
Singing Glory to God as praise filled the skies
For the audience of lowly shepherd's eyes.

Arrested by glory and bathed with the light
In the presence of God that pierced the night.
The news brought us joy as heaven drew near
When the angel proclaimed, our Messiah was here.

We, men of low standing amid ancient hills
Would proclaim God's grace that cleanses and fills.
A statement of love was His advent and birth
He came for the helpless and humble of earth.

We ran to the town, not daring to wait
'Till we found the One that ordered our fate.
We fell to our faces from bended knee
To worship the One who God sent as King.

For a King is born in Bethlehem town
Not in a palace where riches abound.
Born in a stable and laid in a trough
Sent as humble to save the lost.

The God of heaven comes where we are
He's kind and close, not distant or far.
He makes it easy as He draws so close
To the sinful man, He loves the most.

"Therefore it says, "God resists the proud, but gives grace to the humble"
James 4:6 WEB

The Greatest News

It wasn't the rich and powerful ones
Who were blest with the first holy news.
It wasn't the court of the synagogue
Nor the prideful that He would choose.

It wasn't the palace or government seat
Where God sent the angels to say,
That the Savior had come to earth
For us all on that special day.

He sent the word to the humble
The marginalized shepherds of old.
The glorious news was entrusted
To the keepers of the sheepfold.

It's a message within a message
That He came for all of mankind.
No one's exempt from His grace
And all who seek Him will find.

So seek the Lord while He is here
He appears as we humbly bow.
His grace is ours for the taking
Let's give our sins to Him now.

It's not just for a chosen few
We all are made whole through Him,
Through the greatest gift ever given
His love and forgiveness of sin.

"But the angel said to them, "Do not be afraid. I bring you good news that will cause great joy for all the people. Today in the town of David a Savior has been born to you; he is the Messiah, the Lord." Luke 2:10-11 NIV

Prodigal Journeys

For the one who...

is worried if God will accept them.	p.38
made mistakes.	p.39
struggles with a generational sin or curse.	p.40
has intrusive thoughts.	p.42
is tired of the pain.	p.44
needs mercy.	p.46
wants to see God's glory.	p.47
fears they may fail God.	p.48

Prodigal's Song

Have I gone too far and sinned too much?
When I reach for You, will You spurn my touch?
Have I crossed the line never to return?
Will my hopes for grace fade away and burn?

Are You mad at me? Is Your love still there?
If I scream in pain, do You still care?
Can You forgive me once again
This prodigal heart that ran to sin?

I have turned my back so angrily.
My temper flared and blinded me.
As the smoke now fades, I see inside.
I need You, God, to be my guide.

I can't be good without Your help.
Thought I could manage by myself.
But I now see the brutal truth.
That my life is chaos without You.

God, help me now, forgive me, please
I don't want to live without Your peace.
You are holy and void of sin
Through Jesus' blood, You'll let me in.

I want to live to honor Your name;
Not for my will or selfish gain.
I choose to give my heart to You
So I will reflect Your love and truth.

---

*"I, even I, am he who blots out your transgressions,
for my own sake, and remembers your sins no more."*
Isaiah 43:25 NIV

The Wandering Sheep

You look high and low for the wayward sheep
It's my errant soul You so lovingly seek.
Your unbounded grace baffles my mind
As You sweetly reign me in each time.

Help me change my wayward heart
You heal the sin that stops my start.
I'll give to You each step I take
And hope grows as the light of day.

I place my life in Your kind hands
I'll hold the rock in shifting sands.
Forgive my failings and my flaws
For I'm unmoored without Your laws.

Thank You, for forgiving me
For Your love that set me free,
For Your correction that restores;
You freely open gracious doors.

Thank You, for loving this wayward sheep
For searching in places rugged and steep.
You step down from Your mighty throne.
To lead this wandering sheep back home.

"Suppose one of you has a hundred sheep and loses one of them. Doesn't he leave the ninety-nine in the open country and go after the lost sheep until he finds it? And when he finds it, he joyfully puts it on his shoulders and goes home." Luke 15:4-6 NIV

Shaking Legs

Lord, can You please cleanse me?
I lift this problem up to You.
For it has been a part of me
Since my tender youth.

Oh, Jesus, You are loving
You'll be faithful to the end.
I need Your grace; oh, purify
This sin I can't defend.

I give You all my striving
To keep hidden things within.
I trust in Your forgiveness
To free me from this sin.

Cleanse me so that nothing stays
Not even one small part.
Lord, I'll give it to You daily
As I lift to You my heart.

Once I'm living holy
With active faith in You.
I will sing the praises
That Your word is true.

In the messy meantime
With shaking legs, I stand.
Placing both my heart and soul
Into Your loving hands.

For You, oh Lord, are faithful
To what I give to You.
And I will be delivered
As I embrace Your truth.

Thank you, God, my holy Lord
For the grace You've given me.
It's through Your truth and love
That I am cleansed and free.

"So if the Son sets you free, you will be free indeed."
John 8:36 NIV

The Battle of the Mind

The battle of the mind takes place in the spirit
It animates the actions, though I can't see or hear it.
The battle of mind, stoked high by fueled emotion
I'm helplessly adrift upon the stormy oceans.

I try, but I still struggle, and then I start to flail
Like a foundering boat under a rising whale,
But one thing I know, of this, I'm sure,
God's loves my soul, and my spirit's secure.

I take comfort in the hope of my sweet salvation
But I need more of You in my low earthly station.
God, please heal; save my heart and mind
I trust and know You as loving and kind.

My Child

It's a battle, My child, but you have the tools
The sword of the Spirit will break cursed rules.
You're not a victim of your heart and mind
Nor tides and seasons, or perilous times.

Fear not, and stand by My Spirit right now
Look to the goal keep your hand on the plow.
You are not made a snake to writhe in the dust
You're a royal child of a God who is just.

Use My word as a sword to sever the ties
Surgically cut out the stress and the lies.
It will weaken and then start to quake
Stand strong, do the work, choose to be brave.

I give you the tools and the powerful key
To break ties that bind and claim victory.
Abandon your doubts; let My word bring truth
Let it shatter deception and deliver you.

"Therefore put on the whole armor of God, that you may be able to withstand in the evil day, and having done all to stand. Stand, therefore..." Ephesians 6:13 WEB

Wanting It to End

Do I desire heaven's home
Or do I merely want to roam
To fields of green, by waters still,
To have a break from toxic fill?

Do I really want to die
Or do I just hate where I now lie?
I'm paralyzed with labored breath
Trapped and entertaining death.

If it was clear and I could see
The good plans that You have for me;
The joy beyond the doubtful gloom
The life You purposed since the womb.

If today I breathe my last
Will I regret my short-lived past?
Do I want my life to end
Or do I just need my heart to mend?

God, oh help me now, I pray
To see the blessing in this day.
Deliver me from deathly paths
From aligning with the devil's plans.

God, I need this thing to change
It far exceeds a toxic range.
I humbly ask, I need Your help
I can't beat this by myself.

I don't want life to end, I just need a break,
From being caught in anger's wake.
I' stuffing my pain that should be healed
From the devil's plan he thought was sealed.

I feel I'm far out on a limb
Bound with pride and selfish sins.
I give You all the things I lack
And trust Your grace to bring me back.

"He heals the broken in heart, and binds up their wounds."
Psalm 147:3 WEB

Mercy Flows

I have closed that door
And turned that page.
My past won't haunt
With time or age.

The Lord saw all I've
Said and done.
I got His mercy
Through His Son.

I rose by grace
To a life anew.
Redeemed and clean
With sin, I'm through.

He has forgiven
My mounting debt.
I give Him the life;
He saved from death.

His grace flows freely,
I forgive as I go.
I will love as He loved me
I'll let mercy flow.

---

*Blessed are the merciful,
for they will be shown mercy" Matthew 5:7 NIV*

It's No Small Thing

It's no small thing, for an infinite God
To live on earth in a body that's flawed.
From mighty to helpless in a wicked world
To forgive as blows and insults are hurled.

It is no small thing where we are right now
It's no small sin as we follow the crowds.
They called for His death, their anger boiled.
How quickly hearts become embroiled.

It is no small thing to stand before Him
To give an account for the acts of sin.
Though He sent a cure to a fallen world
Through His pain, grace was unfurled.

It is no small thing; this guilt and shame
Money and power cannot make that change.
Only He can free from this deadly spot
Through Him, my debt was joyfully bought.

It is no small thing that I owe Him today
For sending His Son to come and pay.
I must allow grace to work in me
So I can become His offering.

It is no small thing for an infinite God
To give us His love, though we are flawed.
It is no small thing to reject His gift
That priceless gift of forgiveness.

"Who is a God like you, who pardons iniquity...He doesn't retain his anger forever, because he delights in loving kindness."
Micah 7:18 WEB

Until You Call Me Home

I trust You with my future
I give to You, my plans.
I know You won't drop
What I put in Your hands.

Anxious thoughts still plague me
When I think of what could come.
Unless You work a miracle
My life could come undone.

Can I handle troubled days
And nights of stormy seas.
When all has dissipated
And I'm left with painful pleas?

My Lord, will I be strong?
Can I keep my faith on fire?
When doubt and sorrow fill my soul
Will I reach for something higher?

What if my faith should fail me
And I begin to sink, not float?
Will I blame You for my troubles
For sleeping in the boat?

What if my faith should waiver
Or I can't trust in Your name?
Will I be forever lost
And forfeit all my gains?

Oh Lord, will You prepare me
For the trials yet to come.
Let me walk in victory
Until You call me home.

"But when he saw the wind, he was afraid and, beginning to sink, cried out, "Lord, save me!" Immediately Jesus reached out his hand and caught him." Matthew 14:30-31 NIV

Love & Friendship

For the one...

who wants to know what love is.	p.50
needs to let go of a toxic relationship.	p.51
needs to know why they don't love you.	p.52
who's concerned for their friend.	p.54
who needs perspective on forgiveness.	p.55
who was misled by others.	p.56
dealing with a snob.	p.58
who struggles with God's acceptance.	p.60
who's temped to argue politics.	p.62

What Love Is

Love is being patient,
Love is being kind.
Love is giving of yourself;
Love is making time.

Love embraces grace
When people seem untrue.
It freely gives to those
Who can't give back to you.

Love gives to a neighbor,
Expecting nothing back.
It humbly reaches down
To fill the pain of lack.

Love is a mighty King
Who forsook a crown and throne.
To rescue us from sin and death,
And to give us heaven's home.

"Love is patient and is kind. Love doesn't envy. Love doesn't brag, is not proud, doesn't behave itself inappropriately, doesn't seek its own way, is not provoked, takes no account of evil; doesn't rejoice in unrighteousness, but rejoices with the truth; bears all things, believes all things, hopes all things, and endures all things. Love never fails". 1 Corinthians 13:4-8 WEB

Rocky is the Bitter Road

Let it go, let it go; you've toiled hard and rightly sowed,
But they can never give you back everything they owe.
With charm, they drew you in and trapped you in your need.
They acted like a savior, but their motive was their greed.

It wasn't fair, you suffered, and you want the world to know
But that won't give you back the innocence they stole.
It feels like you are giving their sins toward you a pass
As they slash and blame you and redefine the past.

They will take your name and run it through the dirt
Turn your loves against you, adding injury to hurt.
They will sow your field with their wicked seeds
That yields heartbreak for you to heal and clean.

The pain runs deep and the loss runs long
They won't have guilt for doing you wrong.
They are broke and cannot pay, it's you who pay the cost.
They don't know how to love or restore what you have lost.

Let it go for your own good; they cannot pay you back.
They will only charge you for a check you couldn't cash.
Get over them, their pool of lies, with venom like the snake
The bitterness is poison that you, not them, will take.

Letting go is not for them; it's for your aching soul
To rid yourself of toxins and move toward being whole.
Let it go, let it go, release the poison, and unload
Let it go, let it go, for rocky is the bitter road.

"Let all bitterness, wrath, anger, outcry, and slander be put away from you, with all malice. And be kind to one another, tender hearted, forgiving each other, just as God also in Christ forgave you."
Ephesians 4:31-32 NIV

You Can't Make Them Love You

You cannot make them love you
No matter what you do.
They may say the words
But it's not a love that's true.

You may get compliance
They may acquiesce for peace,
But you know deep in your heart
They'll leave when you release.

You can't make them love you
Not in a perfect way.
They don't have it in them
To give that love away.

So you can try with all your might
And they might pretend,
But it's an empty victory.
You'll see it in the end.

So, take that strong desire
And give it to the One
Who will stand right by your side
When all has come undone.

For you are loved so perfectly
By One who died for you.
He will never leave your side
His love is always true.

The deepest needs and wants
For love and true acceptance,
Cannot be satisfied within
Earthly love or penance.

It can be filled by One
Who loves you perfectly.
It's only your Creator
Who can fill that unmet need.

"...for love comes from God. Everyone who loves has been born of God and knows God. Whoever does not love does not know God, because God is love." 1 John 4:7NIV

Prayer for My Friend

You came to my mind today;
I felt it in my heart to pray.
That God will bless your life and heart
And let you know He'll not depart.

For troubles make us feel alone,
And unsafe in our own home.
God has walked that road before
For you, He holds hope's open door.

Do not worry or be afraid,
God paved your road of peace today.
He will turn your night to day,
And hear you as you cry and pray.

You aren't alone; He's there with you;
Lift your head to hope renewed.
For you, He'll move the earth and sky
Look to Him for hope and life.

*"The Lord gives strength to his people;
the Lord blesses his people with peace." Psalm 29:11 NIV*

Forgiven

I've walked so many miles, not one in your shoes,
So, who am I to be the judge and jury over you?
Millions of my daily sins, unseen by human eyes
Have all been seen by God, but me, He won't despise.

He gently leads and guides me and cleanses my sins, too.
My faults aren't held against me; I start each day brand new.
So why do I point and stare and raise my eyebrows high?
Why do I revel in your sin and write it in my sky?

Do I forget my million sins God buried in His sea?
Am I so pure I can't forgive when you've offended me?
What's God Almighty think, as He sees my vain attempt
To tally your wrongdoings as fuel for my contempt?

Is He happy and proud of me, or is He angry and appalled?
That I won't give a portion of the grace for which I've called.
Twisted up and mangled, my hands of faith are tied,
In not forgiving you, I've embraced a lie.

Can I expect forgiveness as I ignore what God has done?
Grasping my resentment blocks the blessings of God's Son.
Forgive me, God, and help me see with grace from up above.
Help me give and to receive with the measure of Your love.

"Do not judge, or you too will be judged. For in the same way you judge others, you will be judged, and with the measure you use, it will be measured to you. "Why do you look at the speck of sawdust in your brother's eye and pay no attention to the plank in your own eye?" Matthew 7:1-3 NIV

The Ledge

Oh Lord, I feel abandoned
By those I thought to trust.
Their words are steely swords
With skill, they love to thrust.

Lord, I have been lured
Way out upon a ledge.
When I wasn't looking
They left me on the edge.

They knew the wind would come.
They gave no warning, but instead,
They encouraged me to overstep
And then they quickly fled.

It didn't take a lot, Lord
For me to fall so fast.
I trusted in their false love
That I thought would last.

A denial of their evil
I still am slow to shake.
I think they want the best for me
A mistake I always make.

Oh Lord, they are not like me
I feel like such a fool.
Why can't I seem to understand
That to them I'm just a tool?

A tool to meet their needs
A means to selfish ends.
Give me eyes to see, Lord
That they are not my friends.

Give me a heart of wisdom
And a desire to please just You.
Use this pain to crush my idols
Like only You can do.

"Do not be misled: "Bad company corrupts good character.
1 Corinthians 15:33 NIV

Snobbery Robbery

She looks down her nose at all that is around
To ride high on her horse is her goal and crown.
They are but fruitless trinkets; the things she sees as gold
These riches will be useless when one day she is old.

She doesn't value me since I don't embrace her treasures
To her, I'm a pauper; with her shallow stick, she measures.
Just because she judges and thinks that she's the best
That doesn't mean she is, and it doesn't mean I'm less.

For one day, she'll see wisdom as the scales fall from her eyes
Revealing that she built her kingdom upon lies.
But still begs the question of my hurt and sorrowed heart
Am I willing to forgive her for her demeaning darts?

For she will one day answer for the ways she's injured me
But I must now forgive her since You've forgiven me.
So I place her on Your throne, and I ask You for her healing
That I'll be bound no more by her sharp glass ceiling.

You are just and mighty; I put rejection in Your hands
For I am Your beloved and not who she thinks I am.
I'm chosen, and I'm cherished by the one true King of Kings
And not a soul can change that, no matter what life brings.

So, now it's time to let go of what she thinks of me
And embrace the truth of what God thinks me to be.
For holding to this tightly makes me the judge and jury
Returning hurt for hurt fuels self-destructive fury.

For nothing that she does will change the one I am,
Or the calling of my life that I place in Your hands.
When I hold the pain she causes, I'm the one not free
It will keep me from the grace You have given me.

Lord, heal her of the cause; forgive her for this sin.
I give to You this hurt that she caused once again.
I release her to Your hands; I give to You this pain
I release my bitterness so You can make a change.

"Do not judge, or you too will be judged"
Matthew 7:1-3 NIV

No Love Greater

I've been like this for so long now
Scarcely can I figure out how,
To ease my pain, release my sins
And live with joy from deep within.

Why don't I come as He draws near,
And admit my failures and my fears?
Why do I wait for a new act of God,
When His greatest act was on the cross?

I can choose to put Him off
And bow to human praise and nods.
Or be the one who bows my knee
To flesh's foe: the King of Kings.

But as I ask why did He
Choose to suffer on the tree?
He didn't have to save us all
From our sin and Adam's fall.

Let's not forget a holy God
Had to go where man did trod,
And live our life but perfectly
To be the sacrifice we need.

Blood was spilled; flesh was torn
He bore the heavy crown of thorns.
Jesus suffered willingly
As a substitute for you and me.

No matter what I do or say
Or if I give my life today,
It can't match the love of God
When He died for me upon the cross.

A wooden symbol, the bridge He laid
By His blood, our debt was paid.
He showed us through His painful loss
There's no love greater than the cross.

"For while we were yet weak, at the right time Christ died for the ungodly." Romans 5:6 WEB

Political Divides

There is so much anger
When we take bitter sides.
There's warring within families
Over political divides.

Neighbor hating neighbor;
Friend divorcing friend.
Nothing more is sacred;
And no one makes amends.

How do we let it happen
As we say that we're evolved?
Who exactly benefits
When hurts are unresolved?

Division only weakens
It's in unity we stand.
But we stoke divisive fires
That will burn our land.

Why did we let it happen
Letting discord gain a hold?
Life is slowly stripped away
As love is growing cold.

The enemy of love
Is the author of this hate.
Let's embrace God once again
And get our ethics straight.

"See to it that no one falls short of the grace of God and that no bitter root grows up to cause trouble and defile many."
Hebrews 12:14:15 NIV

Family & Children

Psalms for :

a faithful mother.	p.64
a thankful moment.	p.65
the Proverbs 31 woman.	p.66
celebration of newlywed love.	p.67
a pregnant mother's prayer.	p.68
a mother of young children.	p.69
prayer for a child born in troubled times.	p.70
priority check for the distracted mom.	p.71
one who prays for their prodigal love	p.72

A Touch of Heaven

A touch of heaven in my home;
A lighted path to God's kind throne.
A glimpse of grace from up above,
All came to me through Mom's sweet love.

Her loving hands were soft and worn.
Her tender voice was kind and warm.
Her love so strong with mercy mild;
Revealed the grace of Heaven's Child.

I could believe He died for me
As I see how she loved me.
Her heart ached as I walked away,
Yet she still loved and always prayed.

I brought distress, yet she loved me still
I broke her heart and tested God's will.
Yet prayers and love she ever bore
Though my soul I ripped and tore.

With love, she prayed so faithfully,
As she saw me wreck God's plan for me.
She stood her ground with faith and love
This turned my eyes to God above.

She loved me after all I'd done
I knew through her, God wouldn't shun.
I was a mess, but could believe
That He'd forgive a wretch like me.

I can't repay the debt I owe
But will grow the seeds that she's sown.
I will turn to Him with my debt to pay
And honor God with my life each day.

"You are our letter... known and read by all men... written not with ink, but with the Spirit of the living God; not in tablets of stone, but in tablets that are hearts of flesh." 2 Corinthians 3:2-3 WEB

Given

What's this given on bended knee?
Circle of love
In my destiny.

What is this gift I have in my hands?
A seed of promise
From baby to man.

What is this bundle I hold tenderly?
A precious daughter,
God's gift to me.

What is this breath I'm given to breathe?
A moment to prepare
For eternity.

"Every good and perfect gift is from above, coming down from the Father of the heavenly lights, who does not change like shifting shadows.." James 1:17 NIV

Above Rubies

She's the last to bed
And the first to rise.
She works for her God
And not for man's eyes.

She labors with might
For her family's gain.
She brings good and not harm
Seeks no honor or no fame.

Her God is her strength
The one she must please.
Her heart's in His word
His word is her key.

It's the key to her joy,
Her strength and peace.
It wards off despair,
Doubt and greed.

Her words soothe the heart
Her strength calms the soul.
Her hands are productive
Her works are pure gold.

Her substance, God's spirit
She fears not old age.
Her beauty grows
As time turns each page.

"A wife of noble character who can find? She is worth far more than rubies." Proverbs 31:10 NIV

Newlywed Song

Who is the one who sings
In tune with my lyrical heart?
Whose spirit sings in harmony
Creating love-filled art?

Who opens my heart with his smile?
Who brightens my mind and soul,
Bringing tears to my eyes with his laugh
And warmth where it once was so cold.

Who came and filled my loneliness,
Bringing change from the hand of God?
When he shuts the door, its dark in my soul,
But by who's side I freely trod.

Who lights torches in me with his look
And reflects God's closeness to me?
Who is one who gave me his vow?
It's my love and the only one for me.

My love, Christopher

"How handsome you are, my beloved! Oh, how charming!"
Song of Songs 1:16 NIV

Prayer for My Child

My child of love,
Tender and sweet.
May the grass be soft
Beneath your feet.

May you grow in favor
As you grow in size.
May the light of God
Shine through your eyes.

May the truth expel
All earthly doubt.
May the lion flee
From your tiny shout.

May you find green fields
And fertile ground.
May your ears be filled
With lovely sounds.

May God light your path
May His love be yours.
May you delight in your God
As you walk through His doors.

"And Jesus grew in wisdom and stature, and in favor with God and man." Luke 2:52 NIV

Bloom

Tiny seeds by careful hands
Are planted tenderly.
Watered and protected,
They have so many needs.

Joyous moments in your day,
When the little sprout arises.
Watered with your tears and toil,
Warmed with sweet surprises.

On the watch for weeds
That will come and spoil;
The thief who wants to steal
From your love's great toil.

Everything you sacrificed
And all that you have given.
Are placed inside a seed of life,
That brings the joy of living.

For one day, before you know,
There will be a great surprise.
The beauty of your labor,
Will bloom before your eyes.

"Let's not be weary in doing good, for we will reap in due season if we don't give up." Galatians 6:9 WEB

Child Warrior

Make her (or him) a warrior, I pray
God, lend her Your power and might.
Provide Your angels to protect.
Give her strength to fight.

Gift her with discernment
Lord, open her eyes to see.
While evil is still in the distance
May it go as she prays, "Let it flee."

Let all chains release in her presence
Let no mountain be too high to climb.
May her heart desire You always
May thoughts of love guide her mind.

God, let this precious dear one
Find favor in Your mighty eyes.
May her life be a treasure to You
Unbound by the enemy's lies.

Surround her, God, with your angels
May she always seek the truth.
May she set free all of the captives
May her life be a pleasure to You.

"When the angel of the Lord appeared to Gideon, he said, "The Lord is with you, mighty warrior." Judges 6:12 NIV

Mommy, Do You Love Me?

Mommy, do you love me? It's sometimes hard to tell
I strive for your attention but then you scream and yell.
You spend time on the phone and even with your friends
I am not important, is the message that your actions send.

My hopeful eyes look to you for guidance and support
I often get, "Go play, not now," or some anger-filled retort.
Through your words and actions, I place a value on myself.
How can I feel important, when I'm put daily on a shelf?

Am I supposed to love you back while constantly rejected?
When grown and on my own, I may not act as you expected.
I need an image of myself played out by thoughtful deeds.
Though my needs are small to you, they are big to me.

It's you that I must look to, but one will take your place,
When I want you less and feel the need for private space.
One day, I'll not bug you by tugging at your hip.
Will I value your approval or comfort when I trip?

Is it all that important that it can't wait until I'm gone?
Will you then recall the altars that you sacrificed me on?
They will hardly be a memory, fading deep into the past,
But who I become and how I parent will for generations last.

Please, Mommy, please, I really need you now.
Make the time to be with me; ask God to show you how.

"He will reply, 'Truly I tell you, whatever you did not do for one of the least of these, you did not do for me." Matthew 25:45 NIV

My Prodigal Love

I give You, God, my wayward love
I pray You'd guide them from above,
That You would change all wrong desires
And fill their heart with holy fire.

Give them ears to hear today.
Provide the words I need to say.
Send workers to this darkened field
So they see Your love and yield.

Grow Your grace within their heart.
Let them want a brand new start.
I claim them for Your kingdom plans
Guide them with Your mighty hands.

Heal sin's wounds and evil's pains,
As Godly sorrow brings good gains.
May their heart delight in You.
Let them love Your word of truth.

Protect them in Your holy calling,
As angels keep their feet from falling.
Fill with joy their narrow path.
Spare them from all scornful wrath.

May they hear Your tender voice
And let their broken bones rejoice.
As their once-lost and angry soul
Finds Your love that makes them whole.

"Let me hear joy and gladness; let the bones that you have broken rejoice. Hide your face from my sins, and blot out all my iniquities. Create in me a pure heart, O God, and renew a steadfast spirit within me." Psalm 51:8-10 NIV

Sickness, Death & Heaven

Encouraging words for one who...

needs God in their sickness and pain.	p.74
needs courage to keep fighting.	p.75
is walking through deadly illness.	p.76
just lost a spiritual warrior.	p.78
questions why we die	p.79
prays for one who lost their spouse.	p.80
needs to know their love is in a better place.	p.82
wants to know what heaven is like.	p.83
has a Christian loved one who died.	p.84

Through the Valley (Psalm 23)

Though I walk through the valley of the shadow of death,
I will fear no evil, for I know what God said.
He loves me, protects me; goes before and behind.
I know that my God is mighty and kind.

I walk through the valley; it's dark and bleak.
I will trust in the Shepherd; His voice will I seek.
He guides me with wisdom, with grace He leads.
Though the way is rocky, I have comfort and peace.

When I walk through the valley, He restores my soul
While my unsure feet trod paths unknown.
He will lead to green fields and I'll have my rest
As I walk by still waters, I'll be happy and blessed.

When hard times come and trouble is rife,
I will not fear or get into strife.
For His goodness and mercy will follow me
As He guides me to eternity.

"Surely your goodness and love will follow me all the days of my life, and I will dwell in the house of the Lord forever." Psalm 23:6 NIV

It's Not Over

It's not over 'till it's over
Have hope 'till your last breath.
It's not over 'till it's over
God can conquer death.

Fight the fight with all your might
And just keep getting up,
For the God of the impossible
Will come and fill your cup.

This earthly life will one day fade
All we've treasured will be not.
Each one of us will have our day
To stand before our God.

Through the trials and the sorrows
In all our painful times,
He's as close as our heart's prayer,
And will never leave our side.

It's not over 'till it's over
Your soul's His cherished treasure.
He holds you close and carries you
He loves you beyond measure.

Look up to hope, though weak and frail
Take comfort in this truth.
No matter what you feel right now,
His love will carry you.

---

*"May the God of hope fill you with all joy and peace as you trust in him,
so that you may overflow with hope by the power of the Holy Spirit"
Romans 15:13 NIV*

Walking Through

When I walk through the threat of death
And I can barely catch my breath.
When shadows grow; and block the light,
It's in these times; God fuels my fight.

He doesn't shout from mountains nor light a clouded sky,
Because He walks beside me, my comfort, and my guide.
Scary is the path unknown, when fighting against death.
But my faithful God is here; He gave me life and breath.

Oh God, please breathe Your life, within my weary form.
Let your Spirit conquer the evil of this storm.
I hand You every care and tear; I will not fear tomorrow
You promised to be with me in the joy, pain, and sorrow.

I cannot guess the outcome, but with desperation, pray.
With my mustard seed of faith, I ask for length of days.
I can't praise You in the ground or do what I should do
I cannot live without Your help so I ask my life of You.

Dear Child

Look to Me, My child; I've heard your desperate plea
I'll walk you through this valley; trust and lean on Me.
In your weakness, I am strong; I work miracles, you'll see.
As you cross this raging ocean, keep your eyes on Me.

I'm the lover of your soul, the keeper of your heart.
You asked Me to come in and I will not depart.
Do not fear, My child; give to Me your life.
I'll walk you through the deepest, darkest nights.

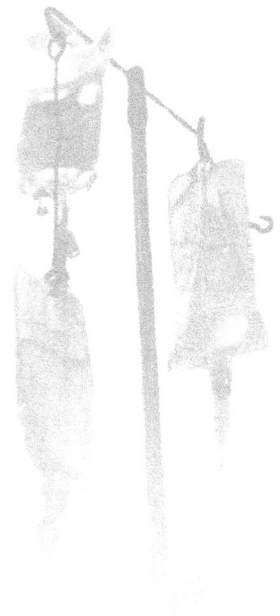

My Chemo I.V.'s

"I will in no way leave you, either will I in any way forsake you."
Hebrews 13:5 WEB

The Good Fight

I have fought a good fight
I have run the good race.
I've carried the torch
Without slowing my pace.

I served with my might
In the power of His word.
I looked only to Him
For eternal rewards.

Like incense that burns
I gave all for my King.
I drowned out my doubt
In the praises I'd sing.

I've been blessed on the earth
With family and friends.
I have comfort and strength
And His love in the end.

As I step from this world
To His arms, so dear.
I'll breathe next in heaven
Without a doubt or a fear.

I get to now see
His magnificent face.
And receive my crown
For a hard-fought race.

I will dance with my God
Without fear or pain.
For He will turn mourning
Into dancing again.

I have fought the good fight, I have finished the race, I have kept the faith. 2 Timothy 4:7 NIV

Live Though We Die

Living in a fallen world
We can't escape the pain,
The evil that is on the earth
The sickness and the shame.

Eden's gates are closed to us,
Adam shut the door.
So, at birth, we're sin-infused
Forever wanting more.

With God, they daily walked
In the coolness of the day,
But for lure of pride and power
They gave it all away.

Then a Savior with the keys
Unlocked heaven's door.
His body was a bridge He laid
Through our sins He bore.

So why do we suffer sickness and pain
And evil forced on weakened frames?
It's the natural growth in the enemy's world
To steal, kill, and destroy are his stated game.

God made a way through His mighty love
To redeem death and bridge divides.
He didn't spare His most precious Son
So we have life though our bodies die.

"He died for us so that, whether we are awake or asleep, we may live together with him." 1 Thessalonians 5:10 NIV

Heaven's Sweet Reunion

Lord, do a tender work
In her dear heart, I cry.
Lord, give her special strength,
Throughout this trying time.

Hold her kind and steadily
Guide her through this sorrow.
Though she feels unready
You hold all her tomorrows.

Heal her aching heart, God,
And guide me in my prayers.
Send people near and far
To show Your loving care.

Surround her with Your love, Lord,
That she won't feel alone.
Bind all thoughts of fear and lack
As You make her heart Your home.

Walk with her each step, Lord,
And sometimes You will carry.
Lord, goodbye is not the end
Of family, love or marriage.

Lord, now be her husband
Walk with her now I pray.
Hold her in Your loving arms
Throughout her grieving days.

Give her joy along the path
That she will walk with strength.
Be her strong and loving guide
Through sorrow's depth and length.

You will walk beside her,
And give her strength and sight.
And one day, when in heaven
She'll rejoice in great delight.

That day, she'll be with You
In heaven's sweet communion,
And she'll see her love again
In heaven's sweet reunion.

"But your dead will live, Lord; their bodies will rise—let those who dwell in the dust wake up and shout for joy—" Isaiah 26:19 NIV

Remember Me

Remember me, don't cry for me
I'm in a better place.
No pain, no tears, no sickness
I'm basking in God's grace.

I have that perfect body
I walk on streets of gold.
I'll see you once again
As we meet in heaven's fold.

Remember me, don't cry for me
Celebrate my God-breathed life.
Remember our good memories
And as God met us in our strife.

Walk away today, and let
His presence comfort you.
Know that He's forgiven me
And He'll forgive you, too.

Let it go; the pain and woe
The sorrow you now feel.
Let the Father comfort you
And allow your heart to heal.

Remember me, don't cry for me
He took my pain and sin.
He will do the same for you
Open up and let Him in.

"The twelve gates were twelve pearls... The great street of the city was of gold, as pure as transparent glass." Revelations 21:21 NIV

Where the Sun Never Sets

Streams of light, songs of color
Warmth and love like no other.
All is at peace; my soul is at rest
In this land of love where the sun never sets.

I walk in pure peace on streets made of gold,
No fear, no pain, no flame, or cold.
I run and laugh, my God ever near,
With His mighty hand, He has dried every tear.

Streams of light, songs of color
Warmth and love like no other.
All is at peace; my soul is at rest
In this land of love where the sun never sets.

Wisdom and light flood my mind
No room for doubt, no worry of time.
I sit at the throne, and I walk with my God
As angels bow low with uplifting laud.

Streams of light, songs of color
Warmth and love like no other.
All is at peace; my soul is at rest
In this land of love where the sun never sets.

"... Lord God Almighty and the Lamb are its temple. The city does not need the sun or the moon to shine on it, for the glory of God gives it light, and the Lamb is its lamp. The nations will walk by its light, and the kings of the earth will bring their splendor into it." Revelation 21:22-26 NIV

Last Breath

There are many mansions
In my Father's house above.
He's been faithfully preparing,
My home with care and love.

So do not be discouraged
Ban fear from your kind soul.
For the One who loves me perfectly
Has come to bring me home.

The hope that I have had in life
Is now the comfort in my death.
And I will place my hand in His
Upon my dying breath.

Do not be discouraged
And do not be afraid.
For I'll live in joy and peace
Because my debt's been paid.

So, my dearest loves
Look up and think of me,
For I will have no earthly pain
And from this earth be free.

I only ask one thing of you
As my final breath draws near.
That you will put your trust in Him
Who takes all sin and fear.

For He has been my strength in life
And now my joy in death.
Accept Him so we'll meet again
On the day of your last breath.

"My Father's house has many rooms... I am going there to prepare a place for you." John 14:2-6 NIV

Salvation Message & Prayer

Dear Reader

It's not by chance that you have this book in your hands. God wants you to know that He sees, knows, and loves you. This world doesn't reflect His love. The venom of sin entered the human race through Adam and Eve. Jesus came to the earth to pay for the curse of sin. He didn't come to be venerated or praised, lauded, or worshipped. He lived a perfect life on earth as a human to become the perfect sacrifice for our sins. If you once had a relationship with Him but have walked away or have never found the beauty of a real and personal relationship with Jesus, this is your moment. Pray this prayer or something like it. Don't let another day pass without the love, forgiveness, help, guidance, and salvation of your Creator.

"Dear Lord, thank You for paying the price for my sins on the cross. I place my sins and mistakes at Your feet right now. Thank You for taking them and casting them into Your sea of forgetfulness, never to be remembered again. Help me to hear Your voice through the Bible. Guide me to live the life You have planned for me. Lead me in the path of Your power and grace, and help me to be a blessing to others. In Jesus' name, Amen."

"Teach us to number our days, that we may gain a heart of wisdom." Psalm 90:12 NIV

If This Book Has Been A Blessing:

Help me get Everyday Matters into the hands of others. Below are a few easy ways.

- Purchase one for a friend or loved one, a get well gift or add to a charity auction basket.
- Mention it on social media. Tag me @sandyryanpopp on Instagram, X, Facebook, or LinkedIn.
- Purchase Everyday Matters for your local hospice, hospital, assisted living facility, pastor or church library.
- Leave a review on Amazon so others can find it. Hover on the QR code below.

Write a review.

Do you know a woman recently diagnosed with cancer?

As a Stage 4 breast cancer survivor, I created The Cancer Prayer Journal for Women—a faith-filled space designed to help women face cancer with courage, clarity, and comfort. With guided prompts to pray, process, and hold fast to hope, this journal offers strength for the journey ahead.

Inside she'll find:

✦ Scripture-based comfort and encouragement

✦ Space for appointments, treatments, and prayers

✦ Pages for your support and medical teams

✦ Reflections, gratitude prompts, and survivor insights

✦ 5-minute writing prompts and calming coloring pages

Available on Amazon.

About the Author

Sandy Popp is a speaker, author, and 10-year survivor of advanced Stage 4 breast cancer. With a powerful testimony of healing, faith, and resilience, Sandy speaks straight to the heart of women navigating life's most brutal battles. Whether walking through illness, burnout, spiritual dryness, or a season of waiting, Sandy brings a message of courage rooted in Scripture and seasoned with grace.

Sandy's journey as a former producer and talent manager has taken her from Hollywood sets to hospital rooms—and, ultimately, into full-time ministry. She is the author of *Everyday Matters: Words of Life*, a devotional poetry collection, and *The Cancer Prayer Journal for Women*, a tool for navigating cancer with intentional prayer. Her blog, *A Cup of Courage*, is a weekly source of encouragement for women seeking God's strength in real-life struggles.

Sandy and her husband Chris have been married since 1988 and have two adult children. Their daughter, Debby Ryan, is an actress, director, and producer who got her big break on Disney Channel's *Suite Life on Deck and* later starred in her own hit series, *Jessie*. Their son, Chase Ryan, is a media producer, photographer, and founder of Ryan River Media.

Sandy offers insight into navigating the entertainment industry with faith, integrity, and balance. Her style is heartfelt, Scripture-rich, and laced with authenticity. In addition to her writing and speaking, she gives historical presentations as a museum educator and enjoys exploring the faith and courage of women throughout history.

She lives in Texas with her husband and loves spending time with their family. Sandy is a passionate prayer warrior, cancer mentor, and lifelong student of Scripture and history.